The Family of
Black America

The Family of
Black America

Text by **Michael H. Cottman**
Photo Editor **Deborah Willis**

RESEARCH BY LINDA TARRANT-REID

CROWN TRADE PAPERBACKS, NEW YORK

The authors gratefully acknowledge the following people and organizations for granting permission to reprint photographs: pages 13–23 by James Van Der Zee, courtesy Donna Mussenden Van Der Zee; 3, 24–29 by Richard S. Roberts, Estate of Richard Samuel Roberts, Collection of Wilhelmina Roberts Wynn; 31–35 by Gordon Parks, courtesy the Library of Congress; 37–40 © Moneta Sleet, Jr.; 1, 41–48 by John W. Mosley, courtesy Charles L. Blockson Afro-American Collection, Temple University Libraries; 50–51 by Juanita Williams; 52 by Eugene Roquemore; 53 by Robert Whitby; 50–53 courtesy Alan Govenar, *Portaits of Community: African American Photography in Texas* (Austin: Texas State Historical Society, 1996); 55 © Stephen Marc; 57–67 © 1996 by Roland L. Freeman, Washington, D.C.; 68–70 © Mel Wright; 71–74 by William E. Lathan, © Bill Lathan; 75–80 Lou Jones; 81–82 Marvin Edwards; 83–89 by Dawoud Bey, 83, 86-89 courtesy Rhona Hoffman Gallery, 84-85 Collection Addison Gallery of American Art; 90–92 Mei Tei Sing Smith; 93 installation by Lonnie Graham in collaboration with the Fabric Workshop, photograph by Will Brown; 94–96 Lonnie Graham; 98–103 by Carrie Mae Weems, courtesy Carrie Mae Weems and the PPOW Gallery, New York City; 105–106 Roland Charles, Black Gallery of Los Angeles; 108–109 © Winston Kennedy; 110–115 © Jeanne Moutoussamy-Ashe; 117–121 © Chester Higgins, Jr. All Rights Reserved; 122–126 Hank Sloane Thomas; 127–131 John Pinderhughes; 132–133 by Radcliffe Bailey, courtesy Fay Gold Gallery, Atlanta; 134–140 Lester Sloan; 141–148 photography by Jeffrey Henson Scales; 149 by David "Oggi" Ogburn, "House of Ogburn" (Photo Archives); 151–156 Accra Shepp; 157–164 Clarissa Sligh; 165–169 Ron Tarver; 170–171 Wendel A. White; 172 Expressly Portraits; 173 Robert Gore; 175 Wendy Nelson.

Copyright © 1996 by Michael H. Cottman

Published by Crown Trade Paperbacks, 201 East 50th Street, New York, New York 10022.
Member of the Crown Publishing Group.

Random House, Inc. New York, Toronto, London, Sydney, Auckland

http://www.randomhouse.com/

CROWN TRADE PAPERBACKS and colophon are trademarks of Crown Publishers, Inc.

Printed in the United States of America

Design by Lenny Henderson

Library of Congress Cataloging-in Publication Data is available upon request.

ISBN 0-517-88822-X

10 9 8 7 6 5 4 3 2 1

First Edition

CONTENTS

If family stories were photographs, I'd need a small museum to house them, but a shoe box could hold all the photos I have of my family.

VERTAMAE SMART-GROSVENOR

INTRODUCTION

Since the beginning of photography in 1839, daguerreans set up studios around the country documenting families in their communities. The role of these early daguerreotypists making family images was important. During those times, few families could afford to have photographs made, but black Americans from cities and rural counties in the North and South, and in the Midwest, Southwest, and West, thought it important to have their family images preserved for posterity.

They began to visit photography studios, where they created idealized portraits of family members. Many studio photographers made images of the family in a formal pose. Most photographs taken in the early years of photography and still existing today were made to commemorate such special occasions in the sitters' life as birthdays, marriage, graduation, holidays, a first dance, military service, wedding anniversaries, and religious ceremonies as well as birth and death.

Later, families began to use photographers to document and preserve an image of their family. As snapshot photography became widespread in the late nineteenth century, a family member was sometimes the designated photographer. Now we can look at family and archival photographs and consider them in a historical context.

Contemporary African-American photographers are beginning to use the family theme as a position from which to create history, to retell stories about the family and the past through images. Family gatherings become photo ops and poignant moments from daily life become immortalized by the lens.

The Family of Black America celebrates visual images and interpretations of family life in America by black photographers between 1900 and 1995. The photographers have different perspectives, but common among them is their ease in telling a story through the photographic medium. Each photographer's image ritualizes the moment, whether it be washing clothes for the family, preparing the family dinner, reading, combing a child's hair, or

7

sitting in a photographer's studio formally dressed.

The Million Man March, held on October 16, 1995, let us salute black family life in America through photographs. Black families still gather in living rooms across the country to reflect on the precious photographs and home videos of proud black men who assembled in the nation's capital for a day of peace and brotherhood. As the anniversary of the Million Man March approaches, those who attended and those who supported the special, spiritually uplifting day will celebrate a day in history never to be forgotten. Our hope is that such a commemoration will help to reinforce family union.

Since the Million Man March, black families have come together for prayer, given time to work in community centers, and set up voter registration drives; and many more have simply spent more time around the dinner table doing what families do best: sharing their love and supporting one another.

As organizers plan for a black-family observance to commemorate the Million Man March on its one-year anniversary, October 16, 1996, black families around the nation are already making advanced preparations to attend the celebration. Husbands and wives are planning their vacation time, weighing their options for transportation, and preparing their children for a historical family gathering. Extended families are talking about ways to come together to preserve the spirit of the Million Man March by participating in a tribute to the largest demonstration in United States history, the largest gathering of black Americans the country has ever witnessed.

This collection of photographs and "word portraits" of black families is meant to fuel the inspiration ignited by the Million Man March for a new emphasis on and redefinition of family and to help us joyously anticipate the day African-Americans are looking forward to—when we can all cherish the legacy of the black family and share in one historic family reunion together.

ONE MILLION MEN
COMMITTED TO
BLACK FAMILIES

s nightfall settled slowly over the U.S. Capitol, a multitude of African-American men who had assembled for the Million Man March offered last-minute handshakes, climbed aboard crowded buses, and returned home to the families who had sanctioned their pilgrimage and blessed their day of spiritual reflection.

For many African-American fathers and husbands, the Million Man March reinforced a commitment to making the family experience work. Proud black men, one million strong, drove across town and across the country to share their day of peace, prayer, and brotherhood with their families; to make good on their pledge to improve the quality of life in their communities; and to keep the spirit of the Million Man March alive in their hearts and their homes.

Echoing through the dark streets of Washington, D.C., were the mighty voices of African-American men chanting "Long Live the Spirit of the Million Man March!" The inspiring, nine-word mantra has come to symbolize camaraderie, spirituality, and

family. It was a chant that shook our souls with a new power that we found deep within ourselves.

They were voices that have been suppressed; voices with passion and purpose that yearned to be heard. And for one remarkable day, October 16, 1995, a nation of loving African-American families listened to a chorus of peaceful voices pledge to respect black women and to bring a sense of spirituality into their living rooms.

As black families spent hours in front of television sets searching for that one familiar face in the crush of black manhood, wives listened to their husbands; children listened to their fathers; sisters listened to their brothers; and mothers listened to their sons. They heard commitment to family, to raise children in the church or mosque for spiritual guidance, to use their strong arms to rock their babies to sleep; to use their rugged hands to dry their sons' and daughters' tears.

Perhaps we were looking for the comfort in the strength of numbers. And in a sense, for that one day, we were all brothers of the soul. We were all family in spirit.

And so one million proud African-American men returned home to one million proud African-American families. Black men went home with dignity. They greeted their wives with long hugs and whispered apologies. Some arrived just in time to kiss their children good-night. Others took a step toward reconciliation with their families simply by walking through the front door.

Black men had come together not only because something was wrong in their lives but also because something was right. Many African-American men were already grounded in the structure of family and wanted to reaffirm, in a very public way, their commitment to family values and their promise to keep their families spiritually enriched.

If there were poignant images to take from the Million Man March, they were of black men who carried their sons high on their shoulders to experience a day of peace and camaraderie among African-American men, a day to expose young people to a peaceful and spiritual demonstration of black male pride. Among the images to preserve were those of African-American men with their wives and children, which underscored the power of the black family. Black families that work can do more than any government agency or social-service organization to help heal our communities.

Black men from coast to coast had assembled to celebrate themselves as well as to express appreciation for black families. In the days that followed, African-American men asked their families to join them in living rooms across the country to spend quiet evenings sharing their extraordinary experiences through home videos, slides, photographs, personal stories, and poignant observations.

The awesome power of that day didn't stop on October 16; it spilled over into the hearts of one million black men and their families who are carrying that feeling, commitment, and energy back into their communities and back into their homes. One year after the Million Man March, perhaps, there are one million African-American leaders, one million black men with one million distinct visions for improving the quality of life in their neighborhoods.

The monumental demonstration signaled an accelerated grassroots movement that is gaining momentum in the same places where civil rights movements in black communities always begin—in church basements, living rooms, and backyards; on front porches; and around dining room tables. Today, an irrepressible spirit from the Million Man March has spawned a quiet power that is blowing across black America like a fresh breeze—from home to home, from block to block, from family to family. An enthusiastic, cross-country alliance among black families and black men is producing new and unlikely leaders every day. College-educated mentors spend Saturdays talking with youngsters about their goals and dreams, helping them to develop their minds along with their jump shots. They are volunteering their time to help keep young black men off the streets, off drugs, and out of trouble.

The Million Man March presented an opportunity to mobilize our families to challenge views that undermine the civil rights achievements that African-American families fought for, protested, and died to win. It has sparked a renewed sense of pride and urgency in many black communities in families of all kinds—two-parent households; single mothers and single fathers; grandmothers who care for their children's children; the uncles, aunts, and other kin in extended families who raise their relatives' babies as their own. All across this country, African-American families have been true to their faith and true to their principles. They have rallied around each other and confronted the social issues that have direct impact on their lives: jobs, housing, racial discrimination, crime, and poverty.

The goals and aspirations of the African-American family today are not so different from those of other families in America: Black families also want safe streets and quality education for their children, affordable and quality housing, a peaceful environment, an equal opportunity for advancement in the workplace, and to provide a loving home for everyone in their family. African-American families have embraced the fundamental values of American society: hard work, strong religious traditions, educating children, a sense of community, civic responsibility, and a dedication to democracy. And since the days of slavery there has been a long, rich tradition of achievement by African-American families even while crosses burned in their yards, while they walked with their children in the sweltering southern sun to boycott segregated bus laws, while they protested together so that we could have the right to vote today.

Black families in America have a history of sacrifice and a tradition of survival. As a people united by a common identity, we cherish our African ancestors and we treasure the accomplishments of each of the black families who came before us. Some families were separated by chains. Members of other black families fought and died on battlegrounds around the world. We pay homage to our courageous forefathers each time we sacrifice our time to help one another.

To honor these great black people, to ensure that we never forget our past, African-American families are leading their children through African-American history museums to pause, reflect, and silently thank our ancestors. African-American mothers and fathers, perhaps as never before, are supplementing their children's education with African-American literature and black multimedia projects, thereby exposing them to a myriad of uplifting stories about black people, black families, and black heritage and providing children with positive—and genuine—portraits of African-American people.

And on steamy summer afternoons in parks, on playgrounds, and near placid lakes across America, black families in record numbers are coming together to picnic on soft blankets, to enjoy fellowship, to trace their roots and study old family albums. At these family reunions young children and great-grandparents join hands in love and say prayers of thanks for generations of strong black people. Perhaps centuries of separation make us cherish our reunions so dearly. Whatever the reasons, reunions have become an integral part of the African-American family experience.

The images of black families in America are broad and varied. These families honor elderly grandparents as our ancestors taught us in the villages of Africa. Parents spend quiet evenings planning for their children's college education or confronting the challenges of raising black boys in urban America. These families are composed of those who are dark-skinned and light-skinned. Some are well-to-do and others are just getting by. Families with two children and families with more than ten are part of these true African-American family images, as are families in which gray-haired grandmothers are raising their children's babies. There are families in which single mothers and single fathers race through the house five mornings a week, tying tiny shoes, tugging on snagged zippers, wiping up spills, and sending their children off to school with hot meals in their stomachs and homework in their hands. These are all families the men of the march celebrate. It is not an aberration, no fluke or chance, that most black families in America are solid citizens, providing loving homes for their children.

There is an aura that connects us as black people and black families, something special in the way we communicate with one another, raise our children, sing, pray, and preach. The grace, diversity, and endless resolve of the African-American family can be seen in these heart-warming photographs of small boys or little black girls, or a black grandmother with years of wisdom etched in her face, or gleeful black families gathered for a day of fellowship for the African-American Family Reunion Celebration.

To acknowledge the countless contributions of black families in America, to witness their tenacity and spiritual strength, to appreciate their depth of intellect and the wealth of knowledge, to comprehend their inner peace after decades of struggles, we only need to embrace every beautiful black person in our own home.

A Mason and his sons, 1926
James Van Der Zee © 1996 by Donna Mussenden Van Der Zee

Right: Father and daughter, 1937
James Van Der Zee © 1996 by Donna Mussenden Van Der Zee

Opposite: Christmas morning, 1933
James Van Der Zee © 1996 by Donna Mussenden Van Der Zee

Below: Tender moments, 1910
James Van Der Zee © 1996 by Donna Mussenden Van Der Zee

The Van Der Zee women and children, Lenox, Mass., ca. 1909
James Van Der Zee © 1996 by Donna Mussenden Van Der Zee

JAMES VAN DER ZEE (1886–1983) was born in Lenox, Massachusetts. He moved to New York City's Harlem and opened his first portrait studio in 1916 on one of Harlem's busiest streets, 135th Street. Van Der Zee is most noted for creating pictorial portraits of the men, women, and children who frequented his studios. Van Der Zee used a number of props to attain a designed effect about the family, among them skillfully painted backdrops that contained images of a fireplace or library, family albums, and cardboard dogs. The legacy of Van Der Zee's years as a photographer lies in the artistic value of his photographs and in his willingness to use his camera in the studio as well as on location, as in the case of photographing his own family outside the family home in Lenox, Massachusetts.

The Van Der Zee men, James, Walter, John, and Charles, ca. 1909
James Van Der Zee © 1996 by Donna Mussenden Van Der Zee

Kate and Rachel, 1909
James Van Der Zee © 1996 by Donna Mussenden Van Der Zee

Sunday morning, 1928
James Van Der Zee © 1996 by Donna Mussenden Van Der Zee

Family portrait, 1928
James Van Der Zee © 1996 by Donna Mussenden Van Der Zee

Father's Day, 1939
James Van Der Zee © 1996 by Donna Mussenden Van Der Zee

Family portrait, 1926
James Van Der Zee © 1996 by Donna Mussenden Van Der Zee

Future expectations (Wedding Day), 1926
James Van Der Zee © 1996 by Donna Mussenden Van Der Zee

Mr. and Mrs. Richard S. Roberts (Dad and Mom), Fernandina, Florida,
ca. 1910. *Estate of Richard Samuel Roberts. Collection of Wilhelmina Roberts Wynn.*

Wilhelmina Roberts at sixteen with oldest brother, Gerald, Columbia, South Carolina
Estate of Richard Samuel Roberts. Collection of Wilhelmina Roberts Wynn.

Five Roberts children and Caesar, 1925
Estate of Richard Samuel Roberts. Collection of Wilhelmina Roberts Wynn.

Richard and Wilhelmina Roberts with their three sons, Beverly, Cornelius, and Gerald, 1914. Fernandina, Florida. *Estate of Richard Samuel Roberts. Collection of Wilhelmina Roberts Wynn.*

RICHARD S. ROBERTS (1881–1936) was active in Fernandina, Florida, and Columbia, South Carolina. He worked as a studio photographer with the assistance of his wife, Wilhelmina. He advertised that his studio took superior photographs by day or night. "To those who desire photographs made of parents and grand-parents but can't persuade them to visit the studio, we say:—Leave them at home. They probably love their home surroundings. Engage us to make that sitting at home. We will respond with pleasure." Robert's own family album pulsates with images of his family: a daughter's "sweet sixteen" portrait, his children waiting to be photographed with friends, as well as a self-portrait with his wife.

Wilhelmina Roberts with parents Richard and Wilhelmina at St. Augustine's College, Raleigh, N.C., 1933. *Estate of Richard Samuel Roberts. Collection of Wilhelmina Roberts Wynn.*

Maternal aunt Vivian Killingsworth and her son Charles, 1924, Columbia, S.C.
Estate of Richard Samuel Roberts. Collection of Wilhelmina Roberts Wynn.

B I G   B R O T H E R

Jalil Akbar, forty, is a security guard at Westminster Presbyterian Church in Detroit, a student at the University of Michigan majoring in education, and a member of the Nation of Islam. What he is most proud of, however, is becoming a Big Brother.

Akbar is intent on having a positive impact on the life of nine-year-old Christopher Stokes. Following the Million Man March, Akbar met Christopher after he joined in the Big Brother/Big Sister mentoring program, sponsored by Westminster Church.

"We go to Pistons and Lions games," said Akbar. "He has opened up to me by sharing peer pressure and school problems."

Akbar never envisioned himself as a mentor, but after the Million Man March he felt "a dire need to get more involved with youth." In addition to helping his "little brother" with homework, he hopes to instill within him with a sense of morality, pride, and self-esteem.

"Society needs to return to the old-fashioned way of taking an entire village to raise one child," Akbar said. "When we were growing up if we did something bad down the street, neighbors would chastise us and when we got home, our parents would be waiting for us, too," he said. "We need to return to the basics of raising our children."

Two brothers, Washington, D.C., November 1942
Library of Congress, LC-USW 3-11082-0

A mother washes clothes in a round tub, Washington, D.C., November 1942
Library of Congress, LC–USW 3-11058C

Mrs. Ella Watson, a government charwoman, with three grandchildren and her adopted daughter, Washington, D.C., August 1942. *Library of Congress, LC-USF 34-13432-C*

A mother preparing dinner in a one-room flat, Washington, D.C., November 1942
Library of Congress, LC-USW 3-11049-C

Grandchildren of Mrs. Ella Watson, Washington, D.C, August 1942
Library of Congress, LC-USF 34-13426-C

Mrs. Ella Watson leaves for work at 4:30 P.M., Washington, D.C., August 1942
Library of Congress, LC-USF 34-13498-C

GORDON PARKS (b. 1912, Fort Scott, Kansas) in 1948 called himself "a reporter with a camera." Parks is noted for realistic style in photographing life in American. In 1942, Parks worked for the Farm Security Administration, photographing, black life in Washington, D.C., among other cities. One of his first assignments was to photograph an African-American cleaning woman in a government office building. Parks spent a great deal of time with her, photographing her at work and at home. Parks's photographs tell a story of the daily lives of hard-working families in Washington, including images of children in their home, a mother preparing dinner, and a dresser adorned with a framed family photograph. The photographs of children are especially touching. Gordon Parks lives in New York City.

OUR FATHERS,
OUR SONS

As the father of four sons, Marlow Henderson believes in sacrificing his time for his family, providing his boys the best education he can afford and countering the negative images of African-American people. He takes his sons to African-American bookstores and museums so they will appreciate the achievements of African-American people.

"Good parenting takes work and sacrifice," said Henderson, forty-four, an auditor with the Department of Defense. Henderson and his wife, Bernice, are raising their children, Marlow III, twenty-three, Corey, eighteen, and sixteen-year-old twins Brian and Bridge, in Baltimore, Maryland.

"You can't be selfish, the kids have to be number one," Henderson said. "Many years we didn't have a vacation because we used the money for activities that would build the boys' character and self-esteem. It was worth the money and the effort."

The Hendersons believe education is the key to their children's success. Marlow III recently graduated summa cum laude from Morgan State University.

Henderson said he is deeply concerned about how African-American families are portrayed by the media. He often asks why the media continues to perpetuate the myth that black families in America are all in the state of crisis.

"We're always put in a negative light," he said. "There's never a balance. It's always who shot whom, never the good stories in our communities to offset the negative."

Father and sons after a day's work in the mines, Superior, West Virginia, 1953
© *Moneta Sleet, Jr.*

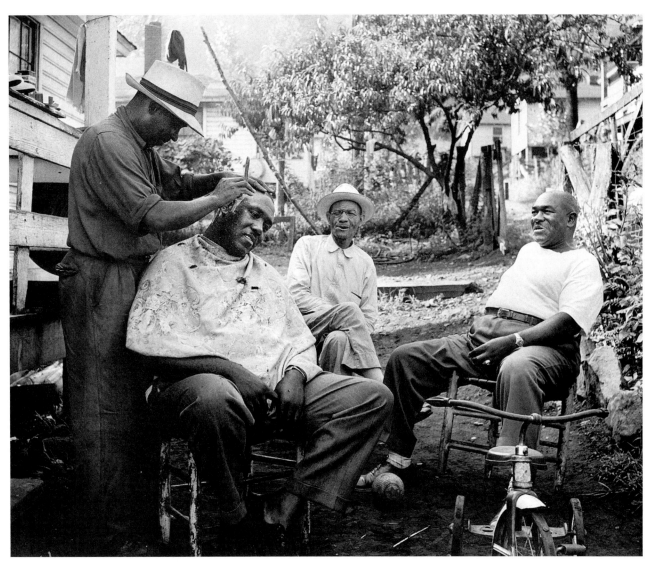

Joe gets a haircut from a neighbor, Superior, West Virginia, 1953
© *Moneta Sleet, Jr.*

MONETA SLEET, JR. (b. 1926, Owensboro, Ky.), has traveled all over the Americas, Africa, and Europe in his long career as a photojournalist. He won a Pulitzer Prize for photography in 1969 for the striking portrait of Mrs. Coretta Scott King with her daughter sitting at the funeral of her husband, Dr. Martin Luther King, Jr. Sleet photographed many families in black America before joining *Ebony* and *Jet* magazines in 1955. This photo essay of life in West Virginia serves as a record of the families who lived near and worked in the coal mines in that state. Life in a rural town in West Virginia is chronicled in the intimate portraits of a young mother bathing her child in a galvanized tub, a father and son walking up a dirt road on their way to church, and a quiet moment on the back porch with the local barber. Moneta Sleet is based in New York City.

Saturday night bath, Superior, West Virginia, 1953
© Moneta Sleet, Jr.

Joe and son Renard on the way to Sunday school, Superior, West Virginia, 1953
© *Moneta Sleet, Jr.*

Dr. William Hamilton's daughters enjoying a birthday treat, Philadelphia, 1944.
Photographs courtesy of the Charles L. Blockson Afro-American Collection, Temple University Libraries;
Photos by John W. Mosley

Children spectators at the Lincoln University–Howard University football game, Philadelphia, 1940s. *Photographs courtesy of the Charles L. Blockson Afro-American Collection, Temple University Libraries; Photos by John W. Mosley*

Judge Raymond Pace Alexander and his wife, Dr. Sadie Tanner Mossell Alexander, with large group, Philadelphia, n.d. *Photographs courtesy of the Charles L. Blockson Afro-American Collection, Temple University Libraries; Photos by John W. Mosley*

Mr. Cannon and grandson, Philadelphia, May 1, 1946

Photographs courtesy of the Charles L. Blockson Afro-American Collection, Temple University Libraries; Photos by John W. Mosley

4 3

Grandmother and granddaughter, "Love and Understanding," Philadelphia, 1945
Photographs courtesy of the Charles L. Blockson Afro-American Collection, Temple University Libraries; Photos by John W. Mosley

Father plays possum with children on a blanket in the park, Philadelphia, ca. 1940s
Photographs courtesy of the Charles L. Blockson Afro-American Collection, Temple University Libraries;
Photos by John W. Mosley

Children at play in backyard, Philadelphia, ca. 1940
Photographs courtesy of the Charles L. Blockson Afro-American Collection, Temple University Libraries; Photos by John W. Mosley

John W. Mosley (center) enjoys taking a self-portrait with his two sons, John W. Mosley Jr. and Charles Mosley, Philadelphia, 1950s
Photographs courtesy of the Charles L. Blockson Afro-American Collection, Temple University Libraries; Photos by John W. Mosley

JOHN W. MOSLEY (1907–1969) was born in Lumberton, North Carolina, and moved to Philadelphia in the mid-1930s. He is best recognized as a chronicler of black life in the Philadelphia area. Many of his family images center on the experience of the black family celebrating birthdays, attending sports events, playing in the backyard, and posing for a photograph. His images create a compelling narrative about the ritual of photographing family expressions. His photographs are in the collection of the Charles L. Blockson Afro-American Collection, Temple University.

Dr. Hamilton's daughter celebrates her birthday with her two sisters and friends, Philadelphia, ca. 1954.
Photographs courtesy of the Charles L. Blockson Afro-American Collection, Temple University Libraries; Photos by John W. Mosley

THE   FAMILY   VOTE

From the moment Rev. Jesse Jackson took the podium at the Million Man March and spoke of eight million African-Americans who remain unregistered to vote, the Banks family decided to make voter registration a top priority. "That number resonated for us," said David Banks, an assistant principal of an elementary school in Brooklyn. "Eight million is far too many of our people to not be involved in the process at all."

Banks, thirty-four, who is married with four children, said that he and his father and two brothers (Philip III, thirty-two, who is a cop; and Terence, thirty, owner of a pest-control business) organized two voter registration drives, one in Brooklyn at Christ Fellowship Baptist Church and another at P.S. 191. Hundreds of people have already registered to vote, Banks said.

While David Banks was growing up, his father was a police officer on the streets of Brownsville, Brooklyn. Philip Banks Jr. saw children's lives being destroyed daily by drugs and drive-by shootings. Determined not to let his three sons end up on the streets, Philip Banks was strict. "Pops was very tough," David recalled, "and my mom was no joke, either." Banks credits his disciplined upbringing for making him a good parent to his own children. "I've always used my parents as the example of how to raise a good family, so raising my own has not been very difficult. Leading by setting a positive example for my children is my way of parenting." David, his wife, Marion, and their children, Jamaal, eleven, Alyia and Ali, six-year-old twins, and Malcom, two, live in Queens.

Banks insists that he is also responsible for all children that he encounters. "We have to be our brother's keeper," Banks said. "It's too dangerous at this point in time for us not to be."

Charles
Johnson

Charles Johnson, Sylvester Johnson, Ronald Craig
Miller, Houston, Texas, ca. 1950
Courtesy Alan Govenar, Portraits of Community: African
American Photography in Texas *(Austin: Texas State
Historical Association, 1996)*

JUANITA WILLIAMS (b. 1926) moved to Houston,
Texas, in 1932. Her sister, Helen, introduced her to
A. C. Teal and his wife, Elnora Teal, who was also a
photographer. After graduating from high school she
studied at the Teal School of Photography from 1943
to 1944. She worked for the Teal Studio as a printer
and darkroom technician until 1951. Williams's photographs are in the collection of Documentary Arts,
Dallas, Texas.

Unidentified couple, Lubbock, Texas, 1950s
Courtesy Alan Govenar, Portraits of Community: African American
Photography in Texas *(Austin: Texas State Historical Association, 1996)*

EUGENE ROGUEMORE (1921–1993) was born in Timpson, Texas. He became interested in photography while he was in the army during World War II. At the end of the war in 1945 he enrolled in Wiley College in Marshall, Texas, and majored in photography. In 1952 he moved to Lubbock, Texas, where he worked part-time as a photographer until his death. His photographs are housed in Documentary Arts, Dallas, Texas.

ROBERT WHITBY

Felicia and Arah Whitby, Austin, Texas, ca. 1951
Courtesy Alan Govenar, Portraits of Community: African American
Photography in Texas *(Austin: Texas State Historical Association, 1996)*

ROBERT WHITBY (1914–1978) was born in Beeville, Texas. He moved to Austin in 1935. During his teenage years he bought a camera and taught himself photography. In Austin, Texas, where he taught Spanish at Anderson High School and Huston-Tillotson College, he worked part-time as a community photographer. His photographs are housed in collections of Documentary Arts, Dallas, Texas.

SAVING OUR BLACK BOYS

The issue facing Angela Dodson and Michael Days of Trenton, New Jersey, was whether to adopt boys. But after visiting a foster home they fell in love with four African-American boys, all brothers.

"The social service supervisor seemed to have a mission to explain the need for the adoption of black boys," Dodson said, "In New Jersey, there are thousands of children waiting for homes, most of whom are black. In almost all cases, parents are looking for girls. There is a perception that boys are difficult to raise. The need for parents to adopt black boys was one of the strongest reasons for us to adopt. If somebody doesn't do something about boys, then our whole society is lost. If our black families don't have boys coming along, then there will not be any black fathers in our next generation."

Dodson sees her children's incredible potential. "We take them faithfully to church every Sunday. We both grew up in the church and spent most of our time in the church, going to all the activities, choir, drama, Bible school, and it had a profound impact on our lives. The boys also get to see our roles in the church. They get to see us taking our place in society. They get to see Michael as the parish president, as well as Daddy; they get to see me in the choir. There are all sorts of role models at the church; there are black men in the choir they look up to; they see very strong black figures every day.

"I'm concerned about safety and the stereotypes that may be dangerous," she explained. "At one store, I sent Adrian back to the car to get my purse and they made him check it at the front. Going into stores with four black boys, we're always being followed. When they leave home, they're out on the street and for society's purposes, they don't look any different than the thugs." Raising her boys means explaining stereotypes and racism to them. "I don't want them to grow up thinking everyone is a racist, but I don't want them to think that there aren't any racists, either. Black men have a rougher road; people automatically see them as a potential problem the minute they walk through the door. Kids don't understand this yet."

Father and son, Lake Shore Drive, Chicago, 1988
© *Stephen Marc*

STEPHEN MARC (b. 1954, Rantoul, Ill.) has created a masterful study in the African diaspora. Photographed in Ghana, Jamaica, England, and the United States, his images portray a sense of unity that extends throughout the communities he has documented. His image of a father and son exemplies trust and free spirit. Marc lives in Chicago, Ill.

PROTECTING
OUR YOUNG

Gilbert Frazier has never been married and he is meeting the challenge of his life: raising three children in Harlem as a single parent. His two youngest children, Sunnn, twelve, and Tolanda, ten, attend a neighborhood Catholic school, where Sunnn is in the gifted program.

"I didn't think I could do this," Frazier said. "Initially I panicked because I didn't know what I was doing. So I had to get my family to help me, I reached out to my family. My mother helped a lot, before she died, but my sister and the kids' grandfather help out now."

Frazier, who works for a telecommunications research firm, said that his extended family is the support network he couldn't do without. They provide the kids with love and another listening ear. He said he's proud to raise them in a black community where everyone looks like them, but he is also aware that the streets of the inner city can have disadvantages.

"I want them to be proud of their culture and proud of being black, because there are forces out there that don't want them to be proud of that or want them to think that everything is homogenized and it's not.

"There's danger in every community and there are dangers here. You teach the kids about the dangers and how to protect themselves, that's all part of being a parent. The more information they have, the more independent they become, they more ability they have to think about who they are and what they want to do and not fall to someone else's criteria, the better their chances are for survival," he said.

Mississippi State Senator John Horhn and Lydia Horhn and their baby, Charla Jade. Jackson, Mississippi, 1992. © 1996 Roland L. Freeman, Washington, D.C.

First National Black Family Reunion on the National Mall, Washington, D.C., 1986
© 1996 Roland L. Freeman, Washington, D.C.

First National Black Family Reunion on the National Mall, Washington, D.C., September 1986;
from left to right, Dorothy Height and three of Dr. Martin Luther King's children
© 1996 Roland L. Freeman, Washington, D.C.

The Earlys: James and Miriam and their sons Ja-Ben and Jah-Mir. Washington, D.C., 1982
© 1996 Roland L. Freeman, Washington, D.C.

Paternal and maternal grandmothers Geleta Clark (left) and Annie Dickerson (right) with Jajaf-Exuma
Thompson, Washington, D.C., 1991
© *1996 Roland L. Freeman, Washington, D.C.*

ROLAND FREEMAN (b. 1936, Baltimore, Md.) has published numerous books on black family life in cities

such as Baltimore, Washington, D.C., and Philadelphia and in rural Mississippi and Georgia and has curated

touring exhibitions to accompany each book. His photographs are intense and sensitive images, a study of

black culture made throughout the African diaspora. Roland Freeman lives in Washington, D.C.

Opposite, below: John Blake, renowned jazz violinist, instructs his three children (Johnathan, Beverly, and
Jennifer) in the musical arts, 1989. John Blake's father established a strong tradition of musical education
within the family. © *1996 Roland L. Freeman, Washington, D.C.*

Above: The Curtis family at supper, clockwise from bottom: Thelma S. Curtis (back turned), Sylvia Williams, Ethel Sadberry, William J. Curtis, Sylvia Curtis, and Tabia Curtis. Detroit, 1986.© *1996 Roland L. Freeman, Washington, D.C.*

Kemba Sonnebeyatta surrounded by her daughter and six sons; clockwise from Cetawayo on her lap, they are Kehinde, Atiba, Hesaam, Sibongile, Obatala, and Taiwo. Philadelphia, n.d.
© 1996 Roland L. Freeman, Washington, D.C.

Preceding pages: The Davis family: Rita and Maceo Sr. with their children, Paige and Maceo Jr. Philadelphia, n.d.
© 1996 Roland L. Freeman, Washington, D.C.

Above: Shirley and Weldon Coleman and their son, Jacob Coleman, Atlanta, Ga., n.d.
© *1996 Roland L. Freeman, Washington, D.C.*
Overleaf: Erinn Cosby, Camille Cosby, Erin Faison, and Ennis Cosby at the twentieth anniversary of the
1963 March on Washington, National Mall, Washington, D.C., 1983
© *1996 Roland L. Freeman, Washington, D.C.*

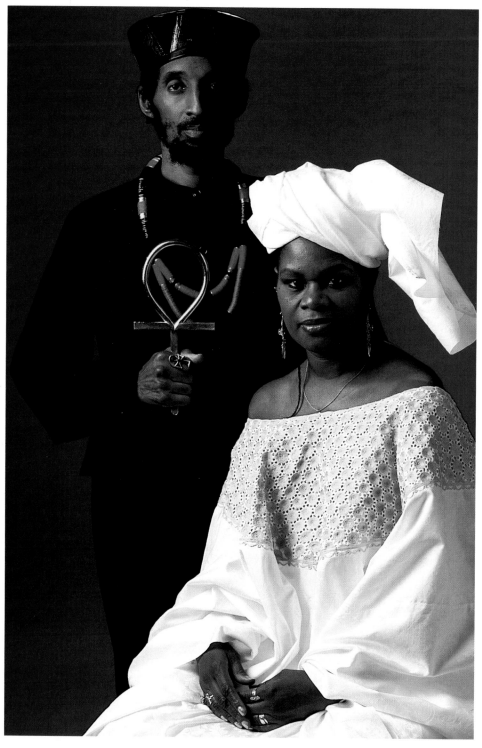

Married couple, n.d.
© *Mel Wright*

Mother and daughter at children's art workshop, n.d. © *Mel Wright*

Mother and daughter—June and Rachel Christmas at a jazz festival, n.d. © *Mel Wright*

American family traveling, Cuzco, Peru—husband-and-wife musical performers, n.d.
© *Mel Wright*

MEL WRIGHT (b. 1942, New York City) photographs families at leisure, informing us of certain aspects of family life that are mostly documented by the family photographer. His images of life in New York, including those of a mother and daughter at a picnic and a young mother reading to her child, share the tranquillity of family life in public places. Mel Wright lives and works in New York City.

Melvina with children Honey, Eddie, and Johnny on 158th and Broadway, New York City, 1975
© *Bill Lathan*

Overleaf: The cousins, Caran, Ginger, Honey, and Medea, family reunion,
Sicklerville, New Jersey, 1991
© *Bill Lathan*

Holman-Foreman family reunion, Ardsley, New York, 1993
© *Bill Lathan*

WILLIAM E. LATHAN (b. 1937, Philadelphia) has documented his family gatherings for the last twenty-five years. Lathan, a passionate observer of the nuances of his family, photographs with candor an afternoon stroll on upper Broadway in New York City and orchestrates a large family reunion portrait to preserve the moment of the gathering. Lathan lives in Ardsley, N.Y.

Father and child visiting a petting zoo, Boston, n.d.
© *Lou Jones*

LOU JONES (b. 1945, Washington, D.C.) photographs families for his commercial work as well as personal projects. Some of his images were made in his hometown of Washington, D.C., on Easter Sunday. Jones also creates stylized images of family reflecting spiritual life and newlyweds, sharing private moments. Jones lives in Boston.

Easter Sunday, Washington, D.C., n.d. © *Lou Jones*

Easter Sunday, Washington, D.C., n.d. © *Lou Jones*

Mother with children after their home was demolished by a storm, Arkansas, n.d. © *Lou Jones*

Family at a Japanese restaurant, Boston, n.d. © *Lou Jones*

Newlyweds, Boston, n.d. © *Lou Jones*

Newlyweds, Boston, n.d. © *Lou Jones*

The Rev. Charles Stith and Dr. Deborah Prothrow-Stith, Roxbury, Massachusetts, n.d. © *Lou Jones*

Family at services, Union Methodist Church, Boston, n.d.
© *Lou Jones*

Dr. Leslie Cooper with her two daughters, Washington, D.C., 1994
© *Marvin Edwards*

Leroy and Shireen Dodson Fykes and family playing Monopoly, Washington, D.C., 1994
© *Marvin Edwards*

MARVIN EDWARDS (b. 1965, Washington, D.C.) captures the life of families in the Washington, D.C., community. Finding a family sharing a game of Monopoly or sitting at home in the living room gives a visual account of the normalcy of day-to-day activities in the home. Edwards lives in Washington, D.C.

Martina and her grandmother, West Side of Chicago, 1994
© *Dawoud Bey*
Courtesy Rhona Hoffman Gallery

DAWOUD BEY (b. 1953, Jamaica, Queens, N.Y.) makes unique studio portraits of families in which each portrait's formal structures are composed by a basic grid. He uses these divisional elements to focus on various parts of the portrait, thereby allowing the viewer to obtain a more intimate visual understanding of his subjects. Bey lives in New Haven, Connecticut.

Martin David, Sara, and Tolani
(Sara Lawrence-Lightfoot and her children), 1992
© *Dawoud Bey*
Collection Addison Gallery of American Art

The James twins, 1992
© Dawoud Bey
Courtesy Rhona Hoffman Gallery

Mary and Louise (my mother and her sister), 1992
© Dawoud Bey
Courtesy Rhona Hoffman Gallery

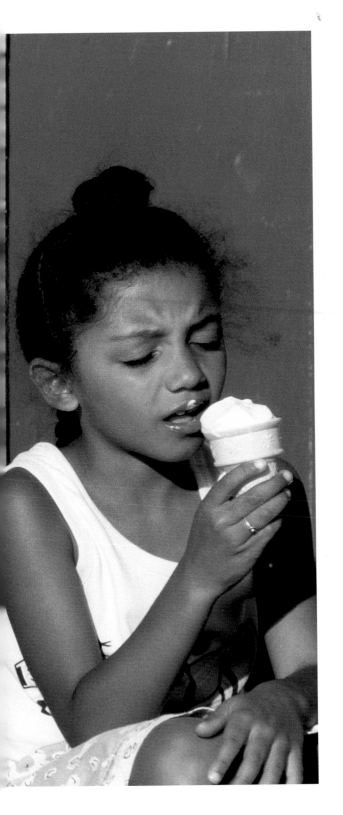

Sing, Larcie, and Bining eating ice cream, Canada, 1989
© *Mei Tei Sing Smith*

MEI TEI SING SMITH (b. 1952, Columbus, Ohio) is a printmaker who uses photography as a document to retain images of her children. For a number of years she has photographed them at play and enjoying quiet moments. The images possess a direct understanding of a mother creating a visual diary of her daughters. Smith lives in New York City.

My daughters, Sing and Bining, 1991
© *Mei Tei Sing Smith*

Living in a Spirit House, Philadelphia, 1994

Installation; Lonnie Graham in collaboration with Fabric Workshop; Photo by Will Brown

Cousins, Michelle and Anthony, Cleveland, Ohio, n.d.
© *Lonnie Graham*

Aunt Dora, Seldom Seen, Pa., n.d.
© *Lonnie Graham*

Uncle Floyd in the garden with a fire, Seldom Seen, Pa., n.d.
© *Lonnie Graham*

L I F T I N G   O U R   S P I R I T S

Rev. Wendell Anthony, pastor of Fellowship Chapel in Detroit, said that several Detroit ministers decided to address the issues of personal responsibility and taking care of family in four sermons from the pulpit immediately following the Million Man March.

"We've been pushing brothers to be responsible; to take care of your families, your babies, your wives," Anthony said. "I didn't try to discourage the grand ideas, but I told brothers not to try to save the nation, just save your family and home and that's one less home we have to be concerned about."

The sermons, Anthony said, apparently had a profound impact on many African-American men in Detroit, who lined up in record numbers to settle their child support payments.

"It was extraordinary," Anthony said. "It was a direct result of the Million Man March."

CARRIE MAE WEEMS

Family pictures and stories. Untitled (Young boy in kitchen), 1979–84
Courtesy Carrie Mae Weems and the PPOW Gallery, New York City

CARRIE MAE WEEMS (b. 1950, Portland, Ore.) is a photographer well known for her photographic series of family pictures and installation art. Weems is a passionate storyteller who is involved with the matrix of family stories. Most of her work records or reflects social and cultural aspects of the African-American family experience. Some of her most reflective work centers around the kitchen table. The kitchen table is, for many of us, the spiritual place for open discussion. The photographs in this book weave stories from the kitchen table to portraits of family and friends sharing moments that connect us to the day-to-day experience in our lives. Carrie Mae Weems lives in New York City.

Family pictures and stories. Untitled (Man with baby), 1978–84
Courtesy Carrie Mae Weems and the PPOW Gallery, New York City

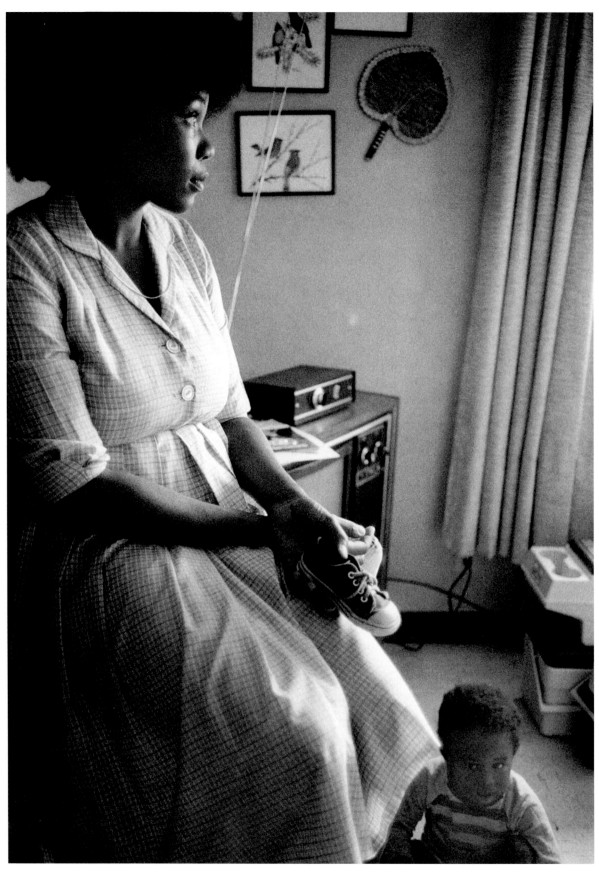

Family pictures and stories. Untitled (Woman in living room), 1979–84
Courtesy Carrie Mae Weems and the PPOW Gallery, New York City

Family pictures and stories. Untitled (Family work together picking beans) 1979–84
Courtesy Carrie Mae Weems and the PPOW Gallery, New York City

My sisters, Van and Vera, with kids in the kitchen
Courtesy Carrie Mae Weems and the PPOW Gallery, New York City

Kitchen table series.
Untitled (Woman with
children), 1990
*Courtesy Carrie Mae Weems
and the PPOW Gallery, New
York City*

T O G E T H E R   A S   O N E

Pamela and Summie Lott, who have always loved large families, see themselves as an extension of the African tradition of incorporating one family into another. They believe in taking personal responsibility for black children who grow up alone in foster homes across the country. The Lotts are the birth parents of two sons: Steven, ten, and Philip, six. They have five adopted children: Freddie, eight; Kenneth, six; Alan, five; Carla, three; and Lloyd, ten months old. Four of the adopted children are biological siblings.

Their first adopted child, Alan, was adopted with the support and guidance of One Church One Child, a national organization dedicated to the adoption of African-American children.

"My husband's mother took in foster kids when he was growing up and when we got married we decided that we would eventually adopt," said Pamela. "Families come together in different ways and we felt that this particular family was meant to be together. I'm filled with joy sometimes when we sit down for dinner. I look at my children's faces and I see that God has brought three families together as one."

Pamela and Summie are both thirty-four, have been married for thirteen years, and live in South Holland, Illinois. Summie is a sales representative for a graphics company. Unlike most parents, they are the primary educators for their children, with school as a supplement. "We look at it as our responsibility to develop self-esteem, values, and morals," Lott said. "Ultimately it falls on us as a family to educate our children."

Pamela, who trains foster parents, has had several discussions with the children's teachers about reinforcing what they are being taught at home. "A lot of times children that come out of the foster care system are viewed as victims. These are my kids and it is important to me that they not be seen that way," she said. "I tell them they were put here because there is a purpose for their life."

ROLAND CHARLES

Pray for Peace, 1990
Roland Charles/Black Gallery of Los Angeles

ROLAND CHARLES (b. 1941, New Orleans) makes photographs of his family and extended family that reveals the domestic nature of the family, whether joined together at a football stadium, at a formal banquet, or on a back porch. His photographs celebrate their ties. Roland Charles lives in Los Angeles.

The Hall family at Danalo Wedding, 1993
Roland Charles/Black Gallery of Los Angeles

The Hall family at the Superbowl in Miami, 1995. *Roland Charles/Black Gallery of Los Angeles*

HARD WORK, HUGS, AND PARENTING

Cynthia Carter, a forty-nine-year-old single mother and public school teacher, is raising her two young boys in New York City. Preparing them for survival in the urban jungle, she says, is crucial. "There is so much in New York that can lead boys astray, especially black boys," Carter said. "We've lost so many kids to drugs, gangs, and alcohol."

Carter said that being a single mother to Omari, fourteen, and Nile, eleven, is quite difficult as she tries to balance her nearly round-the-clock work schedule with giving her boys the direction they need.

"As a single parent I have to be strong, sometimes work two or three jobs just to hold everything together. At the same time I have to separate myself from the boys and not be too overbearing, and that is very difficult for me to do. They are going to be men one day and if I force my way on them, they'll never learn to trust themselves and make their own decisions." The most important activity they do together as a family, Carter said, is coming together for family meetings to discuss the week's events. They review what did and did not work; they talk about chores, activities, and school work.

"On Friday nights we have family night. After waking up early, hustling out to school and work every day, I like us to just relax and do things together as a family. Sometimes we go bowling or maybe rent a movie," Carter said. "On Saturday mornings we make breakfast together. I always prepare something special for them—waffles, pancakes, or fresh-baked muffins. I just realized that this is a family tradition because my dad used to do the same for my sister and me when we were children.

"I don't have a lot of money but I feel what we do as a family will reflect how they turn out as men and eventually how they treat their own families," she said. "The one thing that I've always tried to show my children is that it's okay to spread their love. I'm constantly hugging them and showing them that it's all right to express tenderness and affection," she said.

Mrs. Ella Kennedy, grandmother, at family reunion, Bridgeton, New Jersey, 1971
© *Winston Kennedy*

Family gathering at Curtis and Onella's house. Bridgeton, New Jersey, 1971
© *Winston Kennedy*

WINSTON KENNEDY (b. 1944, Bridgeton, N.J.) documented his family reunion in 1971 in Bridgeton, New Jersey. His image of his grandmother, who is seen as the family historian, is set apart from the other family members seated at a table sharing a meal and pleasant memories. Winston Kennedy lives in Washington, D.C.

JEANNE
MOUTOUSSAMY-ASHE

A ninety-eight-year-old man from Edisto Island with his family
photographs, South Carolina, 1979.
© *Jeanne Moutoussamy-Ashe*

Woman in front of her home with her dogs, Daufuskie Island, South Carolina, 1979
© *Jeanne Moutoussamy-Ashe*

A collection of family memorabilia, Daufuskie Island, South Carolina, 1980
© Jeanne Moutoussamy-Ashe

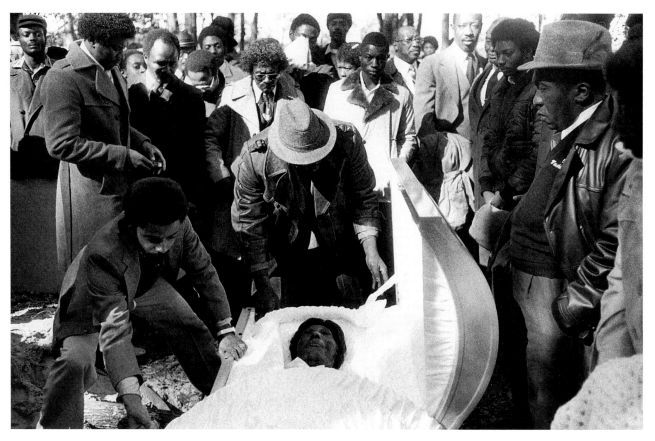

Lavina "Blossum" Robinson's funeral, Daufuskie Island, South Carolina, 1982
© Jeanne Moutoussamy-Ashe

Susie Smith next to a Holy Picture, Daufuskie Island, South Carolina, 1980
© *Jeanne Moutoussamy-Ashe*

Frances Jones, schoolteacher on Daufuskie for 35 years, with her mother, Bell Brown, Daufuskie Island, South Carolina, 1980
© *Jeanne Moutoussamy-Ashe*

Afternoon with Aunt Tootie, Daufuskie Island, South Carolina, 1980
© *Jeanne Moutoussamy-Ashe*

A shrimper and his son, Daufuskie Island, South Carolina, 1979
© *Jeanne Moutoussamy-Ashe*

Washing clothes,
Daufuskie Island, South
Carolina, 1980
© *Jeanne Moutoussamy-Ashe*

JEANNE MOUTOUSSAMY-ASHE (b. 1951, Chicago) has extensively photographed the people of Daufuskie Island in South Carolina. In these particularly revealing photographs she effectively shares a historical collective memory of the families on the island. Her images are informative as she creates a rich visual record of families who display photographs of their loved ones and children in the yard with relatives. She also documents the sense of emotional loss at the funeral of a long-time resident of the island. Jeanne Moutoussamy-Ashe lives in New York City.

G R A N D M A ' S   W O R D S

Juanita Tarrant has seen plenty and learned a lot about child-rearing in her eighty-six years with four daughters, seven grandchildren, and three great-grandchildren, a group of whom attended the Million Man March as a family. She offered wise words. "I have seen a big difference in how kids are raised today," she said. "The whole community used to raise the children, the churches, the neighbors, everybody used to help you. Parents today don't really have anybody to help them. The parents don't even raise their kids, the kids raise the parents."

Tarrant said she focused on education when she was raising her four daughters and she wasn't timid about administering a proper punishment.

"My kids and I had an understanding," she explained. "They respected me and believed me when I said I would do something if they did something wrong. I would spank their behinds or punish them. I don't think parents do that today.

"It's important to put the children in activities—church, Sunday school, scouts, camp. They have to be exposed to what other people are doing so they can learn. There were nine of us. My mother raised us alone. Four boys and five girls, the older two girls worked and gave my mother money to help support us. The boys were young so we took care of them.

"I was married to my husband over forty years. He didn't really participate in disciplining the girls. I did it all. It was important for us to be a complete family even though my husband didn't deal with the nuts and bolts of raising a family. He worked and I took care of everything else."

Great-Aunt Shugg Lampley, Alabama, 1968
Copyrighted photograph by Chester Higgins, Jr. All rights reserved

On the way to church, Alabama, 1972
Copyrighted photograph by Chester Higgins, Jr. All rights reserved

My great-aunt Shugg Lampley prayed every morning and every evening, Alabama, 1968
Copyrighted photograph by Chester Higgins, Jr. All rights reserved

CHESTER HIGGINS, JR. (b. 1946, Bessemer, Ala.), is the photographer and author of the recent book *Feeling the Spirit: Searching the World for People of Africa.* He has been documenting black family life for more than thirty years. His images portray a sensitivity to black family life, whether the family is in the city of New York or in his home state of Alabama. Chester Higgins lives in Brooklyn, N.Y.

My mother and father, Alabama, n.d. *Copyrighted photograph by Chester Higgins, Jr. All rights reserved*

Rabbi Yhoshua Ben Yahonaton and his wife, Leana Yahonaton, Mount Vernon, N.Y., 1989
Copyrighted photograph by Chester Higgins, Jr. All rights reserved

Great-uncle Forth McGowan fishing in a nearby creek with my children, Alabama, 1976

Copyrighted photograph by Chester Higgins, Jr. All rights reserved

HANK SLOANE
THOMAS

A family selling bean pies at the Million Man March, Washington, D.C., 1995
© *Hank Sloane Thomas*

My mom with cousins Caran and Kalia, Rochester, New York, 1995
© *Hank Sloane Thomas*

Graduation Day, my cousin, Mecca Brooks, Rochester, New York, 1995
© Hank Sloane Thomas

Sunday morning, my grandmother and aunt Yvonne leaving the North Penn Baptist Church, Philadelphia, 1995
© *Hank Sloane Thomas*

My grandmother and Aunt Leslie in the kitchen, preparing for a party, Philadelphia, 1995
© *Hank Sloane Thomas*

HANK SLOANE THOMAS (b. 1976, Plainfield, N.J.) is a young photographer who has been photographing his family in Philadelphia as a follow-up to the work of his grandfather, who was an amateur photographer. His images of his cousins, grandmother, and extended family create a linkage to the images he found in his family album. Thomas lives in Washington, D.C., and studies in New York City.

My great uncle Madison and aunt in Virginia, n.d.
© *John Pinderhughes*

The Pinderhughes family reunion—my dad, uncle Charles, and grandmother, n.d.
© *John Pinderhughes*

Sienna and Ghenet Pinderhughes, 1995
© *John Pinderhughes*

JOHN PINDERHUGHES (b. 1946, Washington, D.C.) incorporates commercial photography in the documentation of his family. He is adept at making lighthearted family images in makeshift studios at a family reunion as well as formalized images of his immediate family in the studio. Pinderhughes lives in New York City.

John, Victoria, Sienna, and Ghenet, 1996
© *John Pinderhughes*

The Yearwood and Flipper family with friends, n.d.
© *John Pinderhughes*

Blue Boy, 1995
© Radcliffe Bailey. Courtesy Fay Gold Gallery, Atlanta

Diamond, 1995
© *Radcliffe Bailey*
Courtesy Fay Gold Gallery, Atlanta

Grace, 1995
© *Radcliffe Bailey*
Courtesy Fay Gold Gallery, Atlanta

RADCLIFFE BAILEY (b. 1969, Bridgeton, N.J.) integrates photographs with old doors and wood frames, creating very complex surfaces, color, and content. Bailey's photo art transcends standard imagery in family portrait making by using old photographs to create memorials to loved ones within home-like familiar structures. Bailey lives in Atlanta.

A father with his two sons, Pasadena, Calif., 1989.
Photo © Lester Sloan

Combing hair, North Philadelphia, n.d.
Photo © Lester Sloan

LESTER SLOAN (b. 1942, Detroit, Mich.) creates journalistic images of black families in urban America that are remarkable because of the wide range of subjects preserved. Sloan states, "These pictures reflect some of the joy, pain, and reality of our sojourn in America." His photographs constrast the more difficult realities of homeless life on the streets of Los Angeles to enshrined images of family life in cities such as Philadelphia. Sloan lives in Los Angeles.

Extended family, North Philadelphia, n.d.
Photo © Lester Sloan

Homeless man with his child, 1993.
Photo © Lester Sloan

The Hunter family, Leatrice, Latasha, Latoya, Charnette, and Frederic, in Los Angeles, n.d.
Photo © Lester Sloan

Twin brothers on Graduation Day, n.d.
Photo © Lester Sloan

Kenny and Kenny Jr., Harlem, 1995
Photograph by Jeffrey Henson Scales

Publisher Earl G. Graves and his three sons, New York City, 1995
Photograph by Jeffrey Henson Scales

JEFFREY HENSON SCALES (b. 1954, San Francisco) photographs with affection the ordinary scenes of every-day life. In photographing his family members at a reunion, other families on the streets of New York, and stylized portraits of well-known figures, he captures unique moments of human interaction, creating a wonderful photographic document. Scales lives in New York City.

American Gothic, New Orleans, 1993
Photograph by Jeffrey Henson Scales

Untitled, 1995

Photograph by Jeffrey Henson Scales

Monie Love with her daughter, New York City, 1993
Photograph by Jeffrey Henson Scales

Adam Clayton Powell Jr. Blvd. and 115th Street, New York City, 1991
Photograph by Jeffrey Henson Scales

Lenox Avenue, New York City, 1987
Photograph by Jeffrey Henson Scales

Scales family reunion, Des Moines, Iowa, n.d.
Photograph by Jeffrey Henson Scales

DAVID "OGGI" OGBURN

Creating "The Family Visitor" newsletter, 1977
House of Ogburn (photo archives)

DAVID "OGGI" OGBURN (b. 1942, Queens, N.Y.) has been the chronicler of his family reunions since the mid-1970s. He created with his family a newsletter, titled the "House of Ogburn," in which he used old family photographs, letters, and interviews to create a family history. Ogburn lives in Washington, D.C.

FROM INMATE TO MENTOR

At twenty-one years old, Michael Gibson has been out of jail for more than two years. He was incarcerated for three years for armed robbery and attempted murder of a police officer.

While in prison, Gibson participated in a weekly prison outreach program called the Black Manhood Training Program. Today, Gibson holds a full-time job as a mentor.

Since the Million Man March, Gibson has been meeting with young men in California prisons and juvenile detention centers, holding workshops and offering them hope and direction after they are released. "After the Million Man March, I decided to become more committed to helping incarcerated teenagers," Gibson said. "I've been very involved in several programs for years, but the march reinforced my commitment."

He is volunteering his time with his own violence prevention program at the San Jose Juvenile Hall, where he speaks and holds workshops twice a month. He addresses issues that include personal responsibility, substance abuse, and helping teenagers resolve their disputes through communication and non-violence. The brotherly spirit of the Million Man March led him to being a friend and brother to other African-American men who are in need of direction.

Deratha and Robin (nephew and uncle), 1990
© *Accra Shepp*

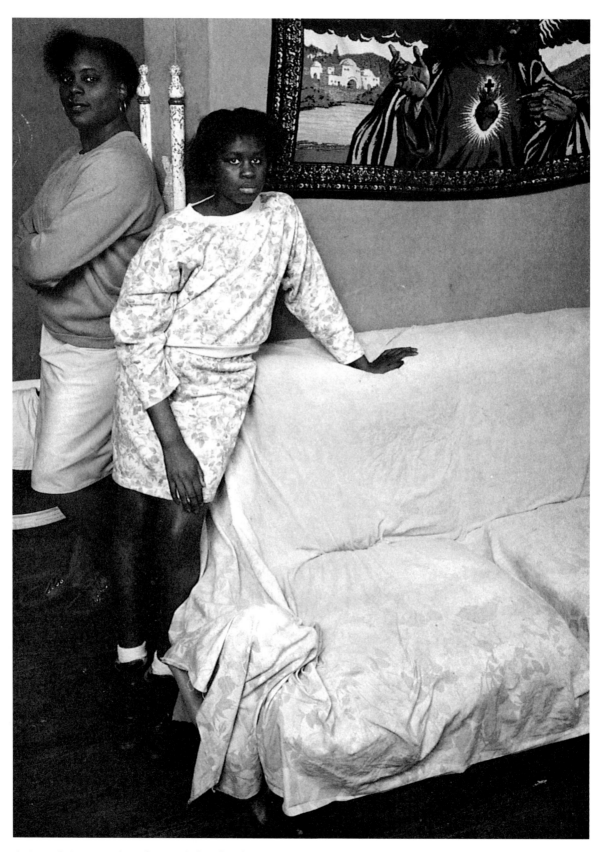

Avis and Antonia (mother and daughter), 1990

© *Accra Shepp*

Living room with family pictures, 1990
© *Accra Shepp*

Colom Street living room, 1990

© *Accra Shepp*

ACCRA SHEPP (b. 1962, New York City) began to photograph his family in Philadelphia in early 1990. The images are of family members on his father's side. In a way of reestablishing family ties, the photographer's project was used to recall stories and family memories that would create a connection from the past to the present. He has photographed relatives at work, in their living rooms, and posing for the camera. Shepp lives in Brooklyn, N.Y., and works in Boston.

Little Jerry in his room, n.d.
© *Accra Shepp*

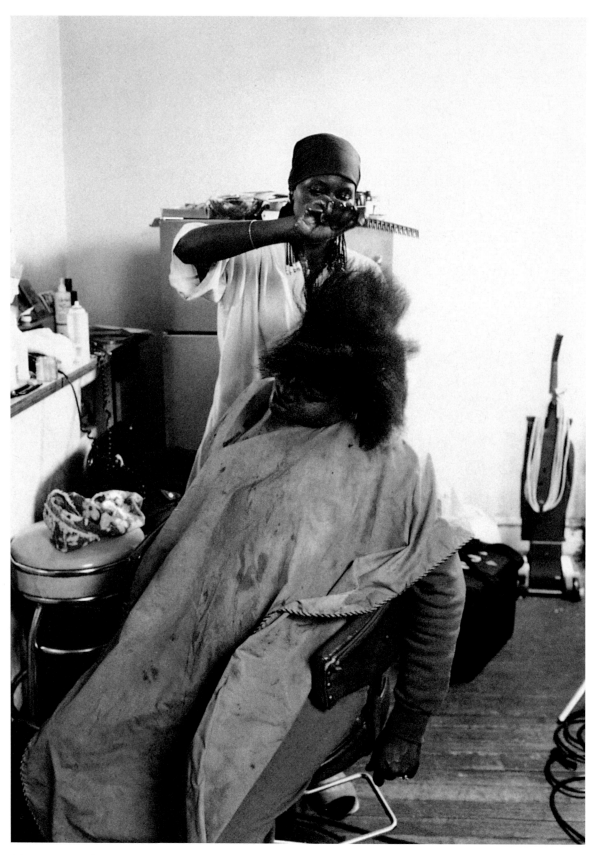

Sharon at work, 1990

© *Accra Shepp*

James C. Watkins with son, Zachary, and daughter, Tighe, Lubbock, Texas, 1995
© *Clarissa Sligh*

CLARISSA SLIGH (b. 1939, Washington, D.C.) creates work that is layered with messages. Using family photographs and text, she directs her audience to gaze into sociological relationships based on experiences in African-American communities past and present. Sligh is the keeper of her family's photograph albums and other memorabilia. She is keenly aware of the role she plays in preserving her family history as she photographs other families. In shifting attention away from her personal experiences, she analyzes shared experiences of other black families across generations. Clarissa Sligh lives in New York City.

Family and porch, Atlanta, 1994
© *Clarissa Sligh*

MY FAMILY HAS BEEN HERE IN GUINNETT COUNTY SINCE THE DAYS OF SLAVERY. MY GRANDMOM STILL LIVES ON THE FARM —BUT SHE SOLD A LOT OF THE LAND ON WHICH THE NEW SUBURBAN HOUSES AND SCHOOLS AND MALLS ARE BUILT. THIS WAS CALLED "THE COUNTRY" WHEN I WAS GROWING UP!!!

Anne Davis with family photographs, Atlanta, 1994
© *Clarissa Sligh*

Mr. Paul R. Jones with photographs, Atlanta, 1994
© *Clarissa Sligh*

Emmanuel Gillespie with daughter, Sagai, Dallas, Texas, 1995
© *Clarissa Sligh*

RON TARVER

Mom and dad in front of house, Fort Gibson, Oklahoma, 1990
© *Ron Tarver*

The haircut. My father had a radio and television business after work that he ran out of a small red building in our yard, we lovingly called it "the shop." He spent nearly every waking moment in the shop or under the large maple shade tree that covered them both. In the fall of 1992 a large wind blew the tree down, crashing into the shop and destroying his business. While his days of television repair had long been over, the tree crashed into more than just a building, it crashed into my father's soul. Six months later he took ill and died. Fort Gibson, Oklahoma

© Ron Tarver

Mom's dresser, #1, Fort Gibson, Oklahoma, 1993
© *Ron Tarver*

Mom's dresser, #2, Fort Gibson, Oklahoma, 1993
© Ron Tarver

Mom's bedroom, Fort Gibson, Oklahoma, 1993
© *Ron Tarver*

RON TARVER (b. 1957, Muskogee, Okla.) has produced wonderful photographic moments of his mother and father at home. The photographing of his family is an extension of the work of his father, who as a hobbiest in the 1940s documented his entire family. The photograph of his mother cutting his father's hair is a poignant moment demonstrating the caring relationship between wife and husband who were married for sixty years. Tarver's father died in 1993. Tarver currently works in Philadelphia.

Margaret Collins

Margaret Collins in the home of her daughter
and son-in-law – Brenda and Eddie Adams. Brenda
and Eddie built their home in Chesilhurst in 1974.

Margaret Collins, Stockton, N.J., 1995
© Wendel A. White

Charles and Pat Amos

Charles and Pat Amos moved to Chesilhurst from Philadelphia in 1966. At the time their children were 2 and 4 years old, they wanted to live outside the city, and land in Chesilhurst was cheap. Charles is a member of the Board of Education and Pat is a Public Health Nurse.

Charles and Pat Amos, Stockton, N.J., 1995
© *Wendel A. White*

WENDEL A. WHITE (b. 1956, Newark, N.J.) has been photographing black families on the southern shore of New Jersey. He interviews families and incorporates text with the photographs, giving the images a sense of attribution and familiarity. White lives in Absecon, N.J.

MICHAEL H. COTTMAN

When I was a boy growing up in Detroit, my mother and father would often remind me to follow my heart and insist that I never give up on my dreams. On Sunday mornings shortly after sunrise, my father would often sit a plate of scrambled eggs in front of me and talk about my responsibil-

sions, dreams, and achievements. This placed my life into a larger historical context, and I felt part of a long line of strong black people, a hard-working black family that overcame racism and economic obstacles to accomplish their many personal and professional goals. My parents insisted that I set my sights high and that they would always support my aspirations.

ity as an African-American man in society, my obligation to give back to our communities. While squeezing oranges for juice, he would discuss the spiritual character and moral strength of the African-American family and the importance of preserving the structure of the black family, a structure that he knew had always been strong, determined, and resilient for centuries.

My father would set the dining-room table every evening while my mother prepared dinner and they would teach me about our family history by flipping through dusty photo albums and faded yellow scrapbooks, walking me through the lives of every black person in those grainy photographs. They would tell me about my extended family—grandparents, cousins, uncles, and great-uncles; their talents, pas-

I followed my heart to the Million Man March. I listened to my father telling me to be proud as I stood shoulder to shoulder among one million black men along the twenty-three-block Mall in Washington, D.C. He wasn't with me physically, but he was there in spirit.

When I close my eyes at night, I can still see a massive assembly of peaceful African-American men standing between the United States Capitol and the Washington Monument, black men with their heads bowed, hands locked and praying in the pre-dawn darkness; black men who stretched across blocks of lawn for as far as the eye could see. I can still feel the support and brotherhood from the Million Man March; I can still feel the breathtaking feeling of connecting with one million familiar souls—

an extended family of African-American men.

Still high from the spiritual intoxication of the Million Man March, I am reminded of the largest demonstration in the history of our country each time I stop to speak or shake hands with other African-American men. I am reminded of the Million Man March each time I see African-American men walking with their wives or bending down on one knee to speak with their small sons and daughters.

I think about my father's astute life lessons over a plate of scrambled eggs and about why my mother felt it so important to teach me about the constellations in the sky. "Why should a little black boy from Detroit care about the stars?" I would ask myself. Because Mom was preparing me to reach for them.

Cottman appears regularly on a weekly New York PBS program, "Informed Sources," a politically oriented round table discussion of top news events. He also serves as an analyst on WRKS-FM's, "The Week in Review," a discussion of timely issues that impact the African-American community. His articles have appeared in Black Enterprise, Essence, Emerge, *and numerous newspapers across the country. Cottman is currently working on a book about the discovery of a seventeenth-century slave ship know as the* Henrietta Marie, *the only slave ship to be scientifically documented, and how a group of African-American scuba divers are confronting their past beneath the sea.*

DEBORAH WILLIS

I remember the first time I saw a book of photographs about black people. It was 1955, I was seven years old. The book by Langston Hughes and Roy DeCarava was *The Sweetflypaper of Life.* It described life in Harlem through the eyes of a grandmother. I was excited to see the photographs. I recognized the people because it reminded me of my family. DeCarava's photographs left me longing for more images about black families and Hughes's lively narration transformed my life at an early age.

Their book led me to ask questions about the photographs we had in our house. The images on the wall, the mantel, and the piano were taken by my father and his cousin, Alphonso Willis. Alphonso Willis was the family photographer and had a

My sister Leslie, me, my mother, and my sister Yvonne in front of "Daddy's Ties," a quilt in tribute to my late father. *Photograph by Robert Gore, 1995*

portrait studio near our house. My father was a serious amateur photographer. His camera fascinated me when I was a child. My father and his cousin were always on hand to photograph special family occasions—graduations, weddings, family reunions, and funerals. They photographed casual gatherings every week. I always looked forward to my father coming home with the past week's prints and negatives. I enjoyed placing the photographs in the photo album.

The Sweetflypaper of Life and photographs in my family album spoke of pride in the African-American family—the good times and the bad times. The ordinary stories these photographs tell were alive and important to me and I continue to cherish them. For me, a veil was lifted.

I have worked as a photographer and curator for the last twenty years. During this time I have made art, published books, and organized exhibitions about family and African-American history and culture. Immersing myself in my ancestral stream of visual memories, I have used it as substance in creating and exhibiting photographic images. In curating exhibitions I have found, analyzed, and displayed photographs showing the diversity and depth of African-American life.

In my teaching, I have instructed students in the methods by which images are manipulated to achieve psychological ends. In my own creative photography I produced work that interrogates the conditions of people of color from Palestine to Brazil. My recent images have visualized relationships within the family. The humanistic values of my mother and father have especially influenced my direction and choices. I made it a mission from that day in 1955 to continue to look for books that were about black people and to look at photographs that told or reflected the story of the family in Black America.

The Tarrant-Reid family. Left to right: Juanita Tarrant, Linda, Siad, Stuart, and Gibwa Reid.
Photograph by Wendy Nelson 1996

LINDA TARRANT-REID

Family is no longer an abstract concept to me, I now have my own. Although my parents provided me with a strong foundation of values and traditions, they didn't seem to matter much until I started raising my family.

My husband, Stuart, and I are teaching our children, Siad, 15, and Gibwa, 12, to be independent thinkers, hard workers, honest, loving and supportive. We encourage them to communicate their feelings, good or bad, and to share their joy as well as their sorrow with us. It's very difficult keeping everyone on track with all of the distractions, but family meals, vacations, and visits to relatives are important rituals that we practice to keep the family in touch.

As a freelance writer working out of my home, I am able to be with my children a lot. Transporting them to and from their various activities and constant communication gives me an opportunity to be involved with their lives and for them to be involved in mine.

I believe they are learning by example. And hopefully these lessons will stay with them and they will be able to pass them on.

ACKNOWLEDGMENTS

In preparing this book I have been dependent on the assistance and cooperation of a number of special people. Without their help and permission to reproduce photographs this book would not have been possible. I would especially like to thank the following: Donna Van Der Zee, Moneta Sleet, Gordon Parks, Jeanne Moutoussamy-Ashe, Shirley Solomon, Mark Wright, Elanna Heywood, Deirdre Cross, Shireen Dodson and Steven Cameron Newsome. Marie Brown, Adrienne Ingrum, Lenny Henderson, Kelvin P. Oden, and Richard Myers supported this project from the beginning. I would also like to give shout outs to my late friend and mentor, Joe Crawford, Kellie Jones, Winston Kennedy, Michael Cottman, Vertamae Smart Grosvenor, Leslie Willis, Linda Tarrant-Reid, Melvina Lathan, Mecca Brooks, Wilhelmina Roberts Wynn, Hank Thomas, Carrie Mae Weems, Clarissa Sligh, Carla Williams, Kathe Sandler, and Sharon Howard. For permission to use photographs in public repositories, I would like to thank the Charles L. Blockson Afro-American Collection, Temple University, the Library of Congress, Howard Greenberg and Documentary Arts, as well as all of the photographers for contributing to the success of this book.

Deborah Willis

I would like to thank the following people for their help and support: Stuart, Siad, and Gibwa Reid, Juanita Tarrant, Marie Brown, Adrienne Ingrum, Reverend Brother Kojo Nantambu, Sandy Cooper, Virginia McCrary, and Gwen Hankins.

Linda Tarrant-Reid

I would like to thank my family for embracing me with the black family experience, for teaching me to appreciate the genius of our African ancestors, and for encouraging me to continue the fight for equality the way millions of our black families have fought for centuries. I would also like to thank Josanne Lopez for her tireless efforts in research and interviews along with the invaluable spiritual energy that helped make this book something special and a book that will make all of us proud.

Michael H. Cottman

IF YOU'RE PLANNING TO VISIT
WASHINGTON, D.C.
By Linda Tarrant-Reid

Washington, D.C., is the site of many historic events including the 1963 March on Washington, the Million Man March, and the Black Family Reunion Celebration. If you are planning a vacation or are attending a family event in the nation's capital, you and your family may also want to visit the many historic sites focusing on the contributions of African-Americans in the Washington, D.C., Area and Baltimore, Maryland.

"The Million Man March (October 16, 1995) was like a spiritual, political, and African rebirth for me. It moved me so much, I would just like other people to share that experience. It's still here, it hasn't died, people are energized. Just seeing that many black men in that environment."

MIKEL HOLT, EDITOR,

MILWAUKEE COMMUNITY JOURNAL,

MILWAUKEE, WIS.

The Mall, a twenty-three-block-long grassy park that stretches from the U.S. Capitol Building to the Washington Monument, is rimmed by the Smithsonian Institution, which houses many museums and galleries that trace the history of America and African-Americans.

From the Mall, your family has an easy access to other historical monuments, including the Lincoln Memorial, the Vietnam Veterans Memorial, and many other interesting attractions. Guided walking and bus tours are also available. For information, stop by the Washington Visitor Information Center, 1455 Pennsylvania Avenue, NW, Monday–Saturday, 9 A.M.–5 P.M.

"The awareness of the Million Man March is very high, there are so many people who regret that they did not attend. My son, Askia, 19, attended the march with me. It was the greatest event he ever witnessed in his life. It made a big difference in his life. He was thoroughly overwhelmed."

REV. BROTHER KOJO NANTAMBU,
ASSOCIATE PASTOR,
GREATER PROVIDENCE BAPTIST CHURCH,
CHARLOTTE, N.C.

Whether your family decides to travel by car, bus, train, or plane, the key is planning ahead. The more information you gather in advance—how to get there, where to stay, and how to get around once you arrive—the better time you and your family will have.

by car:

Make sure your car is road-ready. Check the spare tire, oil, brakes, and signal lights. A road emergency kit, including flares, tire inflator, jumper cables, flashlight, and batteries, and a first-aid kit, is helpful in the event you have a problem on the road. To save time and aggravation map out the best route. The American Automobile Association (AAA) offers members Triptiks, a highlighted map of the most direct and convenient route. If you're not a member, it may be worthwhile to join. Other member services include: twenty-four-hour road service, travel ser-

vices, truck rental, discounts, and traffic safety information. For information call, 1-800-JOIN-AAA.

by bus:

Greyhound and Peter Pan Trailways offer bus service from many cities in the United States. Call Greyhound at 1-800-231-2222 and Peter Pan Trailways at 1-800-343-9999 for information.

by train:

Amtrak provides train service from all over the United States. For information and reservations, call 1-800-USA-RAIL.

by plane:

Three airports serve the metro area: Washington National Airport, located near downtown Washington, D.C. (domestic flights only); Dulles International Airport, 26 miles outside of Washington, D.C. (domestic and international flights); and Baltimore/Washington International Airport, 29 miles north of Washington, D.C. (domestic and international flights). All of the airports offer ground transportation, including taxis, shuttle bus service, and rental cars. For more information call Washington National Airport: 703-685-8000, Dulles International Airport: 703-661-2700, and Baltimore/Washington International Airport: 410-859-7100 or 410-859-7032.

WEATHER IN WASHINGTON, D.C.

Washington, D.C.'s weather averages from 40°F. to the 60s in the spring, the high 60s to the 90s in the summer, from the 50s to 60s in the fall, and 30s to 40s in the winter. Summertime is hot and humid; light clothing in color and weight is a good idea. In the cooler months, dress in layers so when it warms up you can shed them. Wear comfortable shoes and carry a knapsack for snacks, drinks, and incidentals.

"The Million Man March was one of the most spiritual and uplifting things that I've ever been a part of. It was uplifting for me personally, because I ran into my son and my brother on the Mall by the Capitol. It was just a powerful thing being among brothers, to meet them, talk to them, shaking hands, inspiring one another, hearing each other's stories and what they are trying to do."

LEONARD KALONJI TATE,
DIRECTOR, TRINITY HOUSE, ATLANTA

WHERE TO STAY

If you're not staying with friends or relatives, Washington, D.C., has a variety of accommodations in a range of prices. To help you find suitable lodging, the Washington, D.C., Convention and Visitors Association publishes a visitors guide, which lists accommodations in the Washington, D.C./Maryland/Virginia area based on weekday rates. For a copy of the visitors guide, call 202-789-7000. For additional information, call the D.C. Committee To Promote Washington at 1-800-422-8644.

WHERE TO EAT

Carrying a knapsack filled with snacks and cold drinks saves time and money. However, if your family is dying for that Quarter Pounder and fries, there are plenty of snack stands and fast food restaurants in and around Washington, D.C., many of them walking distance from the monuments.

GETTING AROUND IN WASHINGTON, D.C.

If your family is using a car to get around Washington, make sure you park in designated areas. You might want to think about taking the Metro (subway) or the Metrobus to the Mall. The Metro stop closest to the Mall is Smithsonian or Federal Triangle (see map). If your car gets towed, call the D.C. Department of Public Works Towing Information at 202-727-9200 or 202-727-9201. For information on bus and subway schedules and routes, call 202-637-7000.

MEETING YOUR RELATIVES AND FRIENDS

If you are meeting relatives or friends, choose a location and time to meet them. To make it easy for you to find them, be sure to select a prominent and convenient rendezvous point.

POINTS OF INTEREST

There are many historic sites of interest to African-Americans in and around Washington, D.C. Baltimore, thirty miles north of D.C., is also rich in African-American history. The following is a listing of some of these sites.

Washington, D.C.

BANNEKER CIRCLE AND FOUNTAIN
L'ENFANT PLAZA NEAR MAINE AVENUE AND WATER STREET, SW

Named after African-American mathematician and astronomer Benjamin Banneker, who designed Washington, D.C., in 1791, with Pierre Charles L'Enfant.

BLACK FASHION MUSEUM
2007 VERMONT AVENUE, NW; 202-667-0744

A collection of antique and contemporary garments designed, made and worn by African-Americans. By appointment. Donations requested.

BLACK HISTORY NATIONAL RECREATION TRAIL
NATIONAL CAPITAL AREA, OFFICE OF PUBLIC AFFAIRS AND TOURISM; 202-619-7222

National Park Service in cooperation with the Parks and History Association. Magnet sites within historic neighborhoods that illustrate black history from slavery days to the New Deal. Sites include:

- **Mt. Zion and Female Union Band Cemeteries in Georgetown, 2515-2531 Q Street, NW**

These two cemeteries honor African-Americans who helped develop Georgetown. In 1842, the Female Union Band, a black benevolent women's association, bought this land as a burial ground for freed slaves.

- **Metropolitan A.M.E. Church in Downtown Washington, D.C., 1518 M Street, NW; 202-331-1426**
Dedicated in 1886, this Gothic structure is adorned with stained-glass windows and a candelabrum donated by abolitionist Frederick Douglass. Open Monday to Saturday, 10 A.M. to 6 P.M. Sunday worship service at 8 A.M. and 11 A.M.

- **Frederick Douglass National Historic Site and Anacostia, 1411 W Street, SE; 202-426-5961**
Cedar Hill, the home of African-American abolitionist, orator, diplomat, essayist, and auditor of the U.S. Treasury. Visitor Center features a film and exhibits on Frederick Douglass's life. Tours available. Open daily 9 A.M. to 4 P.M. (to 5 P.M. from April 15 to October 15). Closed holidays.

- **Howard University and LeDroit Park, 2400 6th Street, NW; 202-806-6100**
One of the oldest historically black colleges in the United States. Located on the campus are the Gallery in the College of Fine Arts, which houses Alan Locke's African collection as well as rotating exhibits. Also the home of the Moorland-Spingarn Research Center, which contains the largest collection of materials

documenting the history and culture of African-Americans. The Moorland-Spingarn Center is open Monday to Thursday, 9 A.M. to 4:45 P.M. Fridays 9 A.M. to 4:30 P.M. and Saturday 9 A.M. to 5 P.M.

- **Mary McLeod Bethune Museum and Archives and Logan Circle, 1318 Vermont Avenue, NW; 202-332-9201**

Housed in the home of Mary McLeod Bethune, founder of the National Council of Negro Women, this is a research center and archive of African-American women's history. Monday to Friday, 10 A.M. to 4:30 P.M.

- **Emancipation Statue in Lincoln Park and Capitol Hill, East Capitol Street, between 11th and 13th Streets, NE; 202-690-5155**

A statue of Archer Alexander, the last slave captured under the Fugitive Slave Law, breaking the chains of slavery while Abraham Lincoln reads the Emancipation Proclamation. Lincoln Park is the site of the Mary McLeod Bethune statue.

EBENEZER METHODIST CHURCH
420 D STREET, SE; 202-544-1415

The site of the first public school for African-Americans, designated as a historic landmark by the D.C. government in 1975. Tours available. Open Monday to Friday, 8:30 A.M. to 3:00 P.M.

DUKE ELLINGTON SCHOOL OF THE ARTS
35TH AND R STREETS, NW; 202-282-1106

A four-year high school that emphasizes the arts

and academics, named for the famous band leader. Monthly tours available. Call for information.

FAMILY TREE OF LIFE STATUE
16TH STREET AND COLORADO AVENUE, NW

Located in Rock Creek Park, adjacent to the Carter Barron Amphitheater, is a fifteen-foot totem representing an African-American family by Dennis Stoy, Jr.

MARTIN LUTHER KING MEMORIAL LIBRARY
901 G STREET, NW 202-727-1221

Houses special collections on Washingtonian and African-American studies. A mural of Dr. Martin Luther King, Jr., by Don Miller is in the lobby. Open daily. Closed on holidays and Sundays during summer.

MALCOLM X PARK
16TH STREET AND FLORIDA AVENUE, NW

Contains thirteen fountains. This beautifully landscaped park was the rallying point for civil rights groups in the late 1960s.

MARCUS GARVEY AND MALCOLM X STATUE
1440 BELMONT STREET, NW

Twelve-foot steel and stained-glass statue by sculptor A. Uzikee Nelson.

A. PHILIP RANDOLPH STATUE
50 MASSACHUSETTS AVENUE, NE

A bronze statue in honor of the founder of the

Sleeping Car Porter's Union and one of the civil rights organizers of the 1963 March on Washington. Located in Union Station, near Gate C.

SMITHSONIAN INSTITUTION
ANACOSTIA MUSEUM
1901 FORT PLACE, SE; 202-287-3306

Exhibitions chronicling African-American history, art, and culture.

CENTER FOR AFRICAN AMERICAN HISTORY AND
CULTURE ARTS AND INDUSTRIES BUILDING
900 JEFFERSON DRIVE, SW; 202-257-2700

Exhibitions of the African-American experience from the national and international perspective.

NATIONAL MUSEUM OF AFRICAN ART
950 INDEPENDENCE AVENUE, SW; 202-357-2700

Features African art. Walking tours available.

NATIONAL MUSEUM OF AMERICAN HISTORY
14TH STREET AND CONSTITUTION AVENUE, NW; 202-357-2700

Includes the exhibit "Field to Factory: African American Migration, 1915–1940." Open 10 A.M. to 5:30 P.M.

Baltimore

AFRICAN-AMERICAN HERITAGE SOCIETY
P.O. BOX 2402, BALTIMORE, MD; 410-728-3837

Conducts four-hour bust tour of black land-marks for groups, by appointment. Bus rental: $150. $6 per person includes lunch.

GREAT BLACKS IN WAX MUSEUM
1601-1603 EAST NORTH AVENUE; 410-563-3404

Wax museum featuring famous African-Americans of the twentieth century, including Marcus Garvey and Paul Robeson. Open Tuesday to Saturday, 9 A.M. to 6 P.M. House may vary. Admission: $5.50 adults, $5 seniors and college students, $3.50 children 12–17, and $3 children 2–11.

BALTIMORE CITY LIFE MUSEUM
800 EAST LOMBARD STREET; 410-396-3524

Performances of historical presentations of African-American life in the city. Open Tuesday to Saturday, 10 A.M. to 5 P.M.; Sunday, noon to 5 P.M. Admission: $5 adults and $3.50 seniors and children 4–18.

COPPIN STATE COLLEGE LIBRARY
2500 WEST NORTH AVENUE 410-383-5977

Houses memorabilia from bandleader Cab Calloway's musical career. The Parren Mitchell Room contains papers belonging to the United States congressman from Baltimore. Open by appointment only.

ENOCH PRATT FREE LIBRARY
400 NORTH CATHEDRAL STREET 410-396-5500

The Maryland Room is the home of an extensive collection of African-American historical and cultural material. Call for hours.

BALTIMORE MUSEUM OF ART
ART MUSEUM DRIVE 410-396-7100

Permanent collection of traditional African art, including masks and sculptures from West Africa. Open Wednesday to Friday, 10 A.M. to 4 P.M. Saturday and Sunday 11 A.M. to 6 P.M. Admission: $5.50 adults, $3.50 seniors and students, and $1.50 children 7–18.

JAMES E. LEWIS MUSEUM OF ART AND SOPER LIBRARY
MORGAN STATE UNIVERSITY, COLDSPRING LANE AND HILLEN ROAD; 410-319-3022

Permanent collection of African and African-American art and memorabilia from historical African-Americans, including educator and statesman Booker T. Washington, tap dancer Bill "Bojangles" Robinson, and explorer Matthew H. Henson, who accompanied the Peary Expedition to the North Pole. Call for hours.

EUBIE BLAKE NATIONAL MUSEUM AND CULTURAL ARTS CENTER
34 MARKET PLACE; 410-625-3880

Home of artifacts, memorabilia, and photographs from the career of composer and jazz musician Eubie Blake. Open Monday to Friday, noon to 4 P.M.

IMPORTANT TELEPHONE NUMBERS

Automobile Association of America (AAA)—
 1-800-JOIN-AAA

Greyhound Bus—1-800-231-2222

Peter Pan Trailways—1-800-343-9999

Amtrak—1-800-USA-RAIL

Washington National Airport—703-685-8000

Dulles International Airport—703-661-2700

Baltimore/Washington International Airport—
 410-859-7100/410-859-7032

Washington D.C. Convention and Visitors Association—202-789-7000

Metro Transportation Information—202-637-7000

D.C. Dept. of Public Works Towing Information—
 202-727-9200/202-727-9201

Emergency—911

Police (Non-Emergency)—202-727-1010

Metro Transit Police—202-962-2121

Metro (Subway) Lost and Found—202-962-1195
 Travelers' Aid—202-546-3120

FOR MORE INFORMATION

Discover Washington, D.C., from the D.C. Committee to Promote Washington, P.O. Box 27489, Washington, D.C. 20038-7489.

Washington, D.C. Visitor's Guide, from the Washington, D.C., Convention and Visitors Association, 1212 New York Avenue, NW, Washington, D.C. 20005-3992.

National Park Service, Public Information Office, Washingston, D.C. 202-208-4747.

National African-American Leadership Summit and Million Man March Office: 202-726-5111

SOURCES AND CREDITS

Washington Post, Feb. 25, 1996. "In Search of Baltimore's African-American Roots," by Christopher Corbett.

Metrorail System Map reprinted by permission from the Washington Metropolitan Area Transit Authority.

Washington, D.C., Street Map and Washington, D.C., City Map courtesy of Washington, D.C., Convention and Visitors Association.

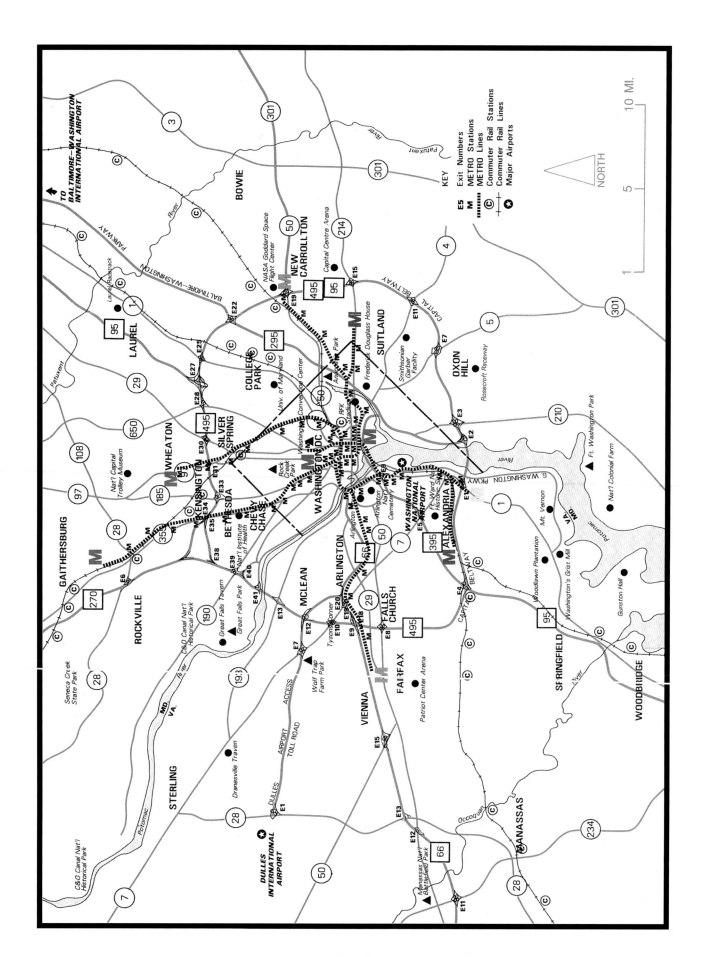

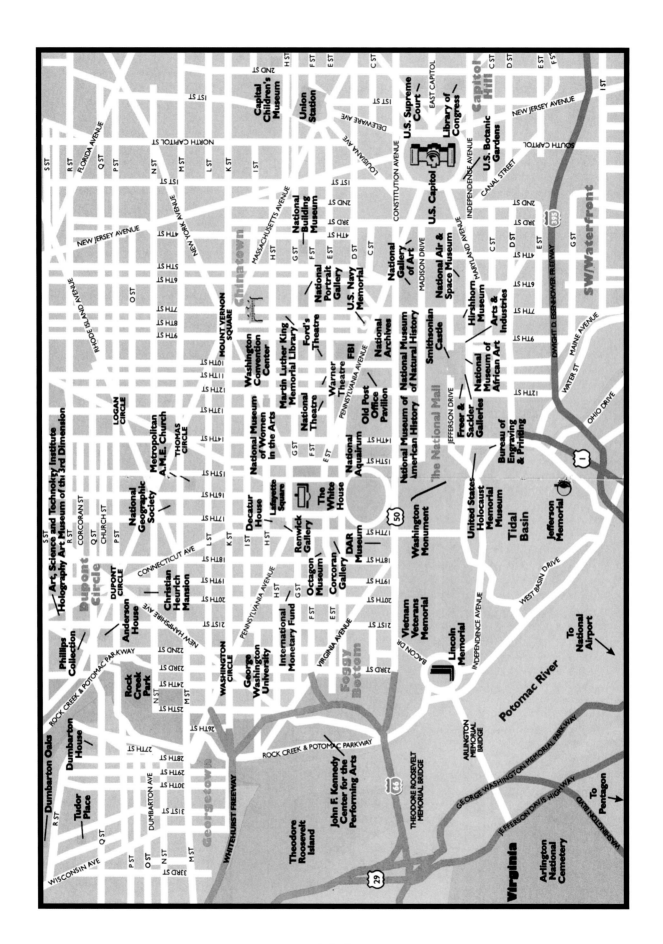

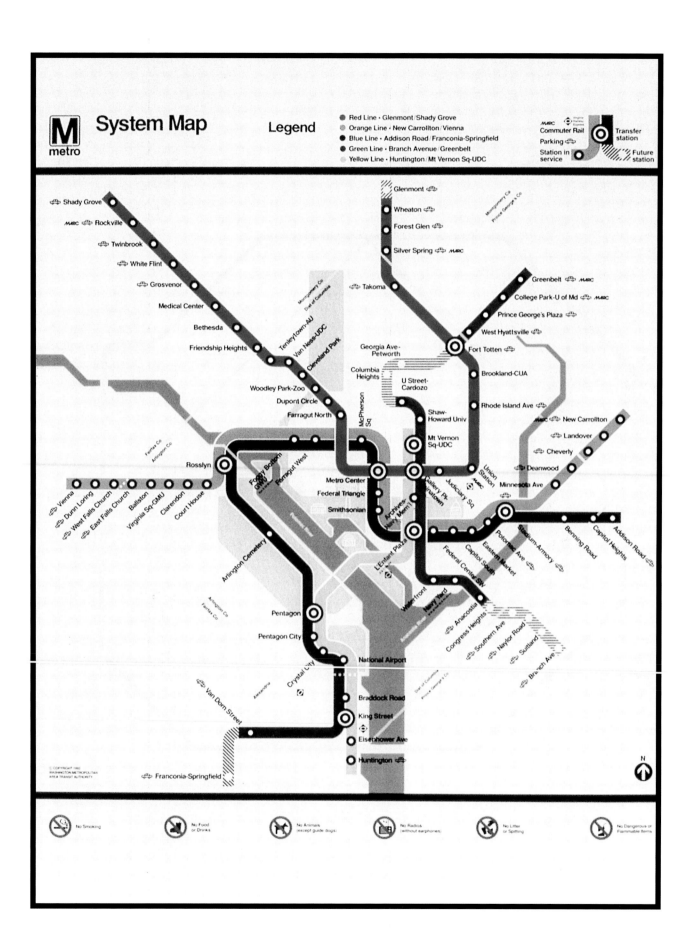

189

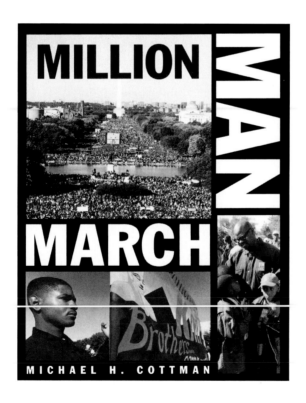

To:

Mrs. Williams

From:

The Tabb Family

Date: 2016

Published by Christian Art Publishers
PO Box 1599, Vereeniging, 1930, RSA

© 2015
First edition 2015

Cover designed by Christian Art Publishers

Images used under license from Shutterstock.com

Scripture quotations are taken from the *Holy Bible,* New International Version® NIV®.
Copyright © 1973, 1978, 1984, 2011 by International Bible Society.
Used by permission of Biblica, Inc.® All rights reserved worldwide.

Scripture quotations are taken from the *Holy Bible,* New Living Translation®.
Copyright © 1996, 2004, 2007, 2013 by Tyndale House Foundation.
Used by permission of Tyndale House Publishers, Inc., Carol Stream, Illinois 60188.
All rights reserved.

Scripture quotations are taken from the *Holy Bible,* Contemporary English Version®.
Copyright © 1995 by American Bible Society. All rights reserved.

Scripture quotations are taken from the New King James Version.
Copyright © 1979, 1980, 1982 by Thomas Nelson, Inc. Used by permission.
All rights reserved.

Scripture quotations are taken from THE MESSAGE. Copyright © by Eugene H. Peterson,
1993, 1994, 1995, 1996, 2000, 2001, 2002.
Used by permission of Tyndale House Publishers, Inc.

Printed in China

ISBN 978-1-4321-1335-3

16 17 18 19 20 21 22 23 24 25 – 20 19 18 17 16 15 14 13 12 11

COLORING BOOK

A FUN, RELAXING WAY
TO UNWIND

TODAY

is going to be

A GREAT
DAY!

ANTI-STRESS THERAPY
AND BIBLICAL INSPIRATION

CHRISTIAN ART
PUBLISHERS

FOCUS on GOD,
see BEAUTY today.
DEVELOP from the negatives
and CAPTURE the
good times.

You honor me as Your guest,
and You fill my cup
until it overflows. Your kindness
and love will always be with me.

Psalm 23:5-6

God gives wisdom, knowledge, and joy.

Ecclesiastes 2:26

As for
ME & MY
HOUSE
we
will serve
THE LORD

Joshua 24:15

Whatever you do,
do all to the glory
of God.

1 Corinthians 10:31

The *will* of God
will never take you
where the *grace* of God
will not *protect* you.

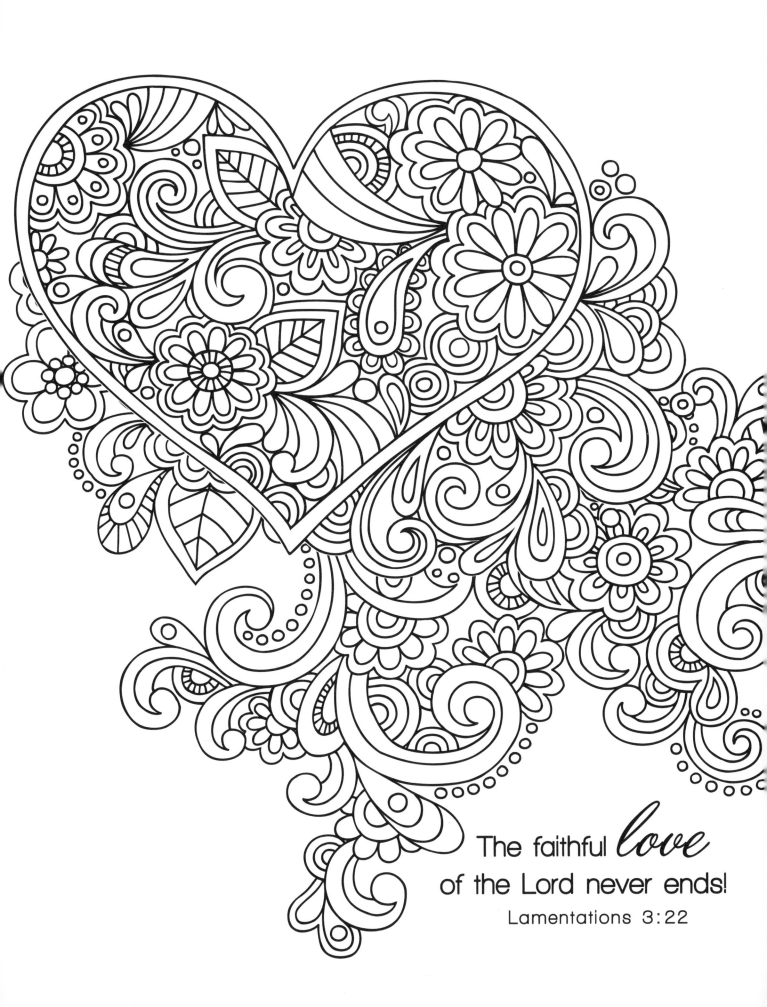

The faithful *love* of the Lord never ends!

Lamentations 3:22

Above all
LOVE
each other
deeply.

1 Peter 4:8

Bloom where God plants you!

Blessed is the one who trusts in the Lord. Jeremiah 17:7

The sun does not shine
for a few trees and flowers,
but for the wide world's joy.

Henry Ward Beecher

Sing
of the LORD's
great love
forever.

PSALM 89:1

A sweet friendship

refreshes the soul.

Proverbs 27:9

Give thanks to the LORD, for He is good.

Psalm 118:29

Love
always protects,
always trusts,
always hopes,
always perseveres.
1 Corinthians 13:7

Love never fails.

1 Corinthians 13:8

*Rejoice in the
Lord always.*

Philippians 4:4

FOLD

Give thanks to the Lord,
for He is good.

Psalm 118:1

Rejoice in the Lord always!

Philippians 4:4

Love never fails.

1 Corinthians 13:8

FOLD

I always thank
my God for you.

1 Corinthians 1:4

I pray that God will greatly
bless you with kindness,
peace and love!

Jude 2

Every time I think of you,
I give thanks to my God.

Philippians 1:3

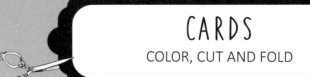

The Lord bless you and keep you.

Numbers 6:24

You have
a special place
in my heart.

Philippians 1:7

May you be
filled with joy.

Colossians 1:11

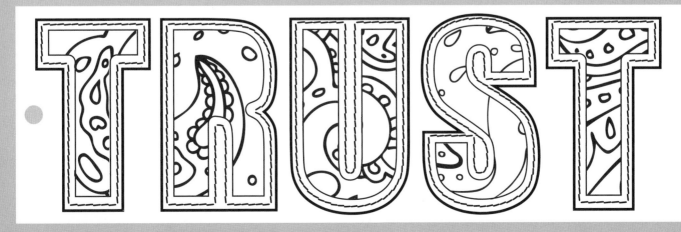

BOOKMARKS
COLOR, CUT, PUNCH & TIE A RIBBON

Today is a GOOD DAY TO HAVE A GOOD DAY

GOD will bless YOU WITH peace GALATIANS 6:16

Trust IN THE LORD WITH ALL YOUR Heart PROVERBS 3:5

WHERE God GUIDES He PROVIDES

GIFT TAGS
Color, cut, punch, tie a ribbon
and write your own special message.

GIFT TAGS
Color, cut, punch, tie a ribbon
and write your own special message.

GIFT TAGS
Color, cut, punch, tie a ribbon
and write your own special message.

GIFT TAGS
Color, cut, punch, tie a ribbon
and write your own special message.